A House for Today

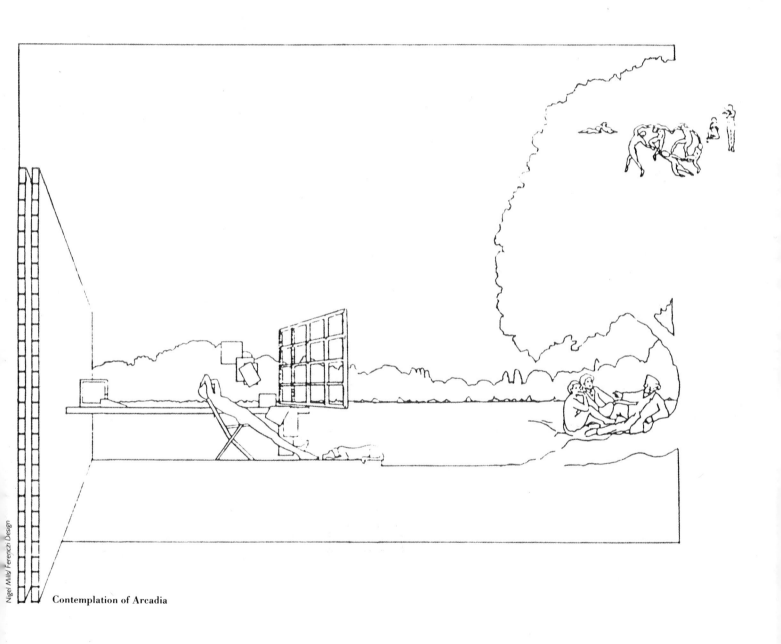

Nigel Mills/ Ferenczi Design

Contemplation of Arcadia

STUDY FOR BEDROOM

BEDROOM

STUDY FOR BEDROOM

AXONOMETRIC NORTH-WEST.

DINING ROOM FROM KITCHEN

BEDROOM STUDY

AXONOMETRIC MASONRY WALLS.

AXONOMETRIC INTERNAL WALLS

PLAN

A.D. Architectural Design Profile 64

A House For Today

BARRATT

A Major International Competition
Organised by Architectural Design Magazine
Sponsored by Barratt Developments PLC

Editor: Dr Andreas Papadakis

First published in Great Britain in 1986 by Architectural Design
AD Editions, 7 Holland Street, London W8

AD Profile 64 is published as part of Architectural Design Volume 56 10/11-1986

Distributed in the United States of America by
St Martin's Press, 175 Fifth Avenue, New York, NY 10010

ISBN 0-312-00713-2 (USA)
ISBN 0-85670-911-5 (UK)

Printed in Great Britain by GA Pindar & Son, Ltd, London

EDITORIAL

OVER THE LAST YEAR, ARCHITECTS FROM MANY different cultural backgrounds have been united in a search for the 'House for Today', a goal with an almost mythical quality. This important international competition has been organized by *AD* with the financial backing of Barratt Developments plc, in order to promote a serious re-evaluation of architectural standards in public housing; and the enthusiastic response, high quality, and enormous variety of entries provide the most convincing proof that the goal set be entirely capable of concrete realisation.

It is a sad fact that the small-scale house has been seriously neglected during the post-war decades, largely because chronic shortage has led the public to snatch up whatever housing it can lay its hands on. However, a wind, or at least a draught, of change has been stirring over recent years, with alterations in the market forcing house-building companies to turn a more receptive ear to sensitivities of demand. The combination of these commercial factors with a move in architectural circles to discard Corbusian ideals of housing for something more homely had created an especially timely moment for the announcement of the competition; and a particularly sympathetic climate for the flowering of results.

It would be wrong to apply a general castigation to all housing development companies; but equally wrong to pretend that a concerted effort to promote thought about this particular sphere of architecture was not long overdue. The root of the problem should probably be located in the complacent approach which has simply failed to see that this term 'architecture' applies as much to public housing as to the creation of the most glorious civic hall or complex cathedral. Thus denigrated to art-less status, public housing has suffered the indignity of being treated as little more than a building exercise; and therefore it is of particular importance that the initiative for this event should have come from a journal known for its publication of the latest currents of thought in architectural design and for its organisation of varied competitions. This in itself should serve to draw attention to the event among architects and housebuilders.

The brief formulated by *AD* took into account criteria laid down by Barratt for a commercially viable move-up house – one that might be an addition to the 20 or 30 house-types that constitute the company's premier range. It asked competitors to put together designs for a detached house, with optional variants for semi-detached, terraced or courtyard forms, and a total floor area of 75m². The house was to be tailored to the needs of a family of four, but with a premium laid on adaptability, so as to accommodate family size changes over the years, if necessary. The budget allocated was £21,000.

With a total of £5,000 allocated for prizes, and the possibility of execution of the winning designs by Barratt, the competition attracted some 250 separate entries from over 20 different countries including Canada, China, Russia, and a number of Eastern bloc countries. Of these, one submission, from Nigel Mills & Ferenczi Design of Portsmouth, was chosen as overall winner, while ten further entries were selected for commendation.

The panel of eight Assessors – Lady Kennet (Chairman), Sir Lawrie Barratt, Dr Alice Coleman (Director of the Land-Use Research Unit), Terry Farrell and Michael Hopkins (architects), Dr Andreas Papadakis (editor of *AD*), and Demetri Porphyrios (architect and critic) – produced a portfolio of comments on each submission which makes clear the simplicity and elegance, fresh quality, or capacity to delight, of the designs. One of the most striking aspects of the various entries was the strong leaning toward the classical in almost all of them; certainly a comment on the revival of interest in classicism in our time. It would seem that so far as the majority of the architects was concerned, the timelessness and familiarity of classical forms and features recommended themselves without rival as the soundest basis upon which to erect a genuine 'house for today' – that is, a house that is really valid for all time. Perhaps it was this ambition to create something really lasting – something much more than the hastily put together living unit of the average modern housing estate – that accounts for the 'poetry' of many of the entries, commented on by the jurors.

However, over-emphasis of this quality did lead some architects into the trap of inadequate working-out of practical requirements in the plans. The competition undeniably threw up a mass of only half-formed ideas; but it should be stressed that really it was this generation of wide-ranging thought and experimentation that was the most important aspect of the event – which is why such a large selection of the designs is here being published. By contrast, inadequate architectural input in the case of another corpus of entries was a more depressing feature; and the jurors noted with disparagement those designs that showed too clearly the hand of the committee or salesman.

It was the desire to promote, as effectively as possible, the character of the competition as an opportunity for the exchange of ideas and experiences that lay behind the organisation of the colloquia which were a unique feature of this competition. Held over three days last spring, these were attended by representatives of various housing-related concerns who came not only to hear, but also to add to, the contributions of four speakers – Terry Farrell, Dr Alice Coleman, Rob Krier, and Mike Norton, of Barratt. These underlined areas felt to warrant particular attention by architects concerned with housing projects, such as the social implication of planning, the entitlement of the individual at every level of society to the possession, in whatever terms, of a home of architectural meaning, and the need to address the limitations of low budget with undimmed inspiration and creativity.

It is too early, as yet, to judge just what the influence of 'A House for Today' will be, or how it will operate. The possibility that the winning designs may be built as a new addition to the housing range remains strong; and the competition was always intended to be of practical use to all housing developers. Essentially, however, it is the 'educational' value of the competition in which the organisers place their highest hopes, and it is most encouraging to hear that a number of architectural schools are now setting the project as a student exercise; for if we are to inculcate a more enthusiastic and committed approach to public housing, both in house-builders and architects, it is here, in the schools that the seeds should be planted.   *ECM*

JOHN MELVIN
Meaning and Metaphor in the Modern House

The Englishman's Dream: An individual house set in an Arcadian landscape loosely tied to a pre-industrial city and invisibly linked to the world beyond by 20th century technology – an impossible idyll as replication erodes those very qualities that give it its unique distinction.

WHEN AN IMMENSELY SUCCESSFUL NATIONAL house-builder, actually building houses for people today, offers to *Architectural Design* the sponsorship of a competition such as this, it is an opportunity for its readers to indulge themselves in a spirit of relaxed good-will and to speculate upon the idea of the house in general.

We are perhaps obliged to approach this task with a degree of playfulness, given the unreality of the brief. However this allows us to free our minds from the contingent and treat the challenge as we would a game, having its own rules and ultimately being its own justification. Being a game it is likely to contain that sense of purposefulness without purpose which Kant took to be the essence of aesthetics. In fact, when we examine those houses which architects have built for themselves, is this not the very quality we find?

Given the enigmatic title of A House for Today, where should a competitor start? Where, in the brief, lies any question from which the architect may derive an answer? Within what constraints can any freedom be found? Where, in the simplicity of our terms of reference, devoid of any particular site or location, can we find a clue, except in some archetype of childhood memory. Here, perhaps, lies the power of Laugier's primitive hut to symbolise both Architecture and Shelter. This image can never be far from our minds when we consider the house *sui generis* or as a thing in itself.

We are not invited to consider the house in any political or social context nor are we asked to dwell on the association of the household, of which the house is the natural expression, with its twin features of production and property, factors that are palpably as much a fact of the household today, as they were for Aristotle and, in more recent times, Hegel. For Aristotle, the household was a location of production, with work being divided into meaningless activity, performed by slaves and productive labour the responsibility of the family. Only if the shuttle should weave itself and the plectrum should do its own harp-playing could slaves and subordinates be dispensed with. Today, the machine has replaced the slave, but with the advent of the home computer and telecommunications, the house is becoming even more a location for production. Recent inflation has underlined most graphically Hegel's claim that in the modern world the house is the embodiment of the idea of property.

The title 'A House for Today' can obviously be divided into two concepts: namely, that of the House and that of Time, ie Today. If we take this latter component to seek a foothold, we find that it gives less support than is initially apparent. Is 'today' forever present suspended motionless between past and future, but with past and future having no meaning? Or are we being asked to consider 'today' as an actual moment, which now incidentally is past? Alternatively, perhaps we are being asked to design a house for the future. Again, this confers a certain degree of unreality to the programme. For any actual building cannot escape the constraints which the past imposes and any leap from these into an unknown future becomes mere sentimentality, where our forms may outrun any supporting idea.

If we turn to the other concept of House, we are almost overwhelmed by the images and thoughts and associations available. Appropriate to the artificial nature of this competition, the idea of the Dolls' House is the first to present itself. A number of the schemes which appealed to the judges had this idealised toy-like character. The dolls' house should have affinity with the house of bricks and mortar and the house of adulthood. But the dolls' house is a lifeless object, a fiction which in our imaginations becomes real. The house, on the other hand is a real object which our imaginations invest with a degree of unreality. The reason for our fascination with *Alice in Wonderland* is that in it we are constantly transported between these two realms of imagination:

Above left: Giulio Romano's own house, Mantua, 1540. One of the first of many architect's own houses. Here the Mannerist game is being played for all its worth. The broken string-course that also becomes a pediment and the window openings that are just too small for the tabernacle frame which they contain are a Mannerist play on the language of Bramante. A game that now once more appears possible; but for the apostate of today, a dangerous one. *Centre:* Soane's own house, Lincoln's Inn Fields. An early proposal for the front facade, showing an arcaded treatment. These neo-classical forms allied to Soane's propensity for funereal imagery anticipate many of the sensibilities of the 20th century. *Right:* Aldo Rossi: the imagery of De Chirico is continued as part-toyland, part necropolis. A departed commedia dell'arte seems to speak of a nostalgia for the past in contrast to the reality of the present, where Pierrot might only come out to dance in the shadow of the incinerator.

the dolls' house which becomes real and the House which becomes dreamlike. We find this in the domestic work of Lutyens and it seems to touch upon the very essence of architectural delight, with logic defying logic, within a framework of reason. This therefore may be a quality which should inform our house today.

Literature abounds in the use of house as metaphor. Dickens invests the house with a personality, as well as it being a mediator for the elements and for mood. Shakespeare on the other hand is able to suggest even the mood of the time of day in Celia's description of her house: "At this hour the house doth keep itself. There's none within." (As You Like It). In Freud's introductory lectures on psychoanalysis we even find him claiming that the house subconsciously is representative of the person as a whole. In our dreams we find ourselves climbing down the facade of a house, enjoying it at one moment, frightened at another. The houses with smooth walls are men; the ones with projections and balconies that one can hold onto are women.

The subconscious, of course, provided 20th century Man with some of his most consoling visions of the house, as he became increasingly lost in a technological world he could neither control nor understand. We find this expressed in the somnambulist paintings of Picasso, in the work of the Surrealists, and most painfully vivid in the work of De Chirico. In his dream-like world of silent cities we can still hear the muffled sob of life, broken only by the scream of a crazed young girl as she chases her hoop through empty squares. The architecture of shadows, arcades and towers has not yet give up its power to haunt, even if the house is now nothing more than a bathing-machine, a contraption of painted canvas and primitive wheels. Innocence has given way to the mere infantile and the toy has become a thing of terror. This is the world of Rossi, to which a number of the entries referred.

If the result of this was an acceptance of a vanished universe, drained of any supporting metaphysic, then some poetry and meaning still seemed possible from the very isolation of Man and his objects. Their very inert dumbness, capable of mindless reproduction, was the impulse of the production-line visions of Gropius, as well as the sanitised abstract minimalism of Hilberseimer, which was accompanied by the thunder of repetition. For Freud this spoke of Thanatos or the death-wish. The death for Gropius was of bourgeois Man and a bourgeois world, where there was no place for the architect, except as technician. The old symbols and forms were now no more than that of their own isolated existence. This was the vision of the *Neue Sachlichkeit*, which when transferred to 'New Deal America' found expression in the paintings of Edward Hopper.

In Hopper's paintings, it is the house that has become the subject and Man one alienated object among others that can find neither support nor consolation. The verandas and porches of his New World bungalows seem opaque to metaphor or meaning and have no life beyond their lonely selves.

In more recent times, even these objects have begun to lose meaning. Reality itself has become unreal under the impact of mass media and commercialisation. Here we enter the world of Post-Modernism and we are faced with either coming to terms with the global village, with its kitsch and its plastic allusions or retreating into a mental construct of our own making. The houses of Eisenman which occupy no position in time or space, and which can be assembled or disassembled in an infinite number of ways, offer one line of retreat and this appeared to be taken up by a number of competitors. Onanistic in its obsession with its own technics and its private fantasies, the Eisenman house can be perceived to be nothing more than a butterfly of the intellect whose life is extinguished the moment it leaves the drawing board.

Do these musings around the poetics of the house have any relevance to the mass house-builder? I believe they do. Some years ago, the economist Fred Hirsch, in a study on the problems

Lutyens, Little Thakeham: picture hall and screen, 1902-3. Here is the 'looking glass' world of Lutyens, where the outside appears on the inside with balconies and rusticated masonry. To emphasise the hearth, the fireplace has a key stone. The relieving arch has an even greater projecting one, above which, where one expects the mass of chimney-breast, we are presented with a projecting balcony and open void.

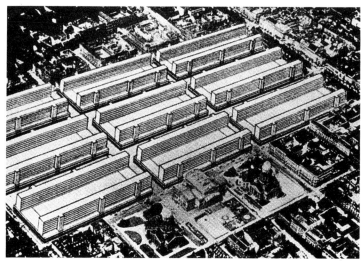

Hilberseimer: a project for central Berlin, 1927. An authoritarian and millenary vision, having much in comon with totalitarianism. The thunder of repetition speaks of death.

Brook Green, West London, John Melvin & Partners. These flats and houses have their meaning reinforced by an emphasis on context and a return to archetype. This is assisted by a nascent modern Mannerism.

confronting developed societies in the late 20th century,* contended that certain patterns of growth could not continue. These were constraints to growth that were social and they impose their own limitations. By this, he meant that while we may have unlimited capacity for the manufacture and consumption of some goods, others by their very nature are limited. These are social or positional goods. Social limits to growth intensify the struggle for distribution, while they increase the importance of relative place. For example, the house on the hill, enjoying both privacy and a fine view, cannot share these advantages without itself losing them.

This is a precise analogue of the ever-running battle between the haves and the have-nots over the issue of the Green Belt. Fred Hirsch also points out that 'private goods have public context in the broad environmental conditions of their use . . .' The public reluctance to see the erosion of the Green Belt stems also from the general realisation that there are social costs which the developer is bound to pass on to the community. In an open market, the developer is obliged to act as a free rider. The market will determine the price of the land, which will not necessarily reflect the true cost of providing the social and economic infrastructure required for its use. The house-builder in the Green Belt hopes to take advantage of proximity to the adjoining city without sharing its burdens. This of necessity is limited and eventually self-defeating, for if he is successful he will end up with neither of the two ingredients necessary for his *rus in urbe*.

It is obvious that these limits have been perceived and that sensibilities are being sharpened for a return to the city, where both infrastructure and supporting institutions already exist: witness the winning designs of Nigel Mills and the Ferenczi Design Group. What conclusions can be drawn from the exercise? Firstly, it has allowed competitors to explore in the widest possible way the architectural poetics of the house, with little constraint or predetermination. Secondly, it has aired the question of meaning and metaphor in the modern house and whether indeed it has any meaning at all. Thirdly, if house-builders are increasingly obliged to turn to the city as they face limits to growth outside the city, they may once again look to architects to give fresh meaning to the house in its totality.

Wittgenstein believes that philosophy begins when language takes a holiday, and that we should not look for meaning in any special idea of meaning, but look for it in daily use. The success of this competition may be just that combination of holiday, with a chance to examine the everyday.

*Fred Hirsch, *Social Limits to Growth*, 1977

WINNING ENTRIES

NIGEL MILLS AND FERENCZI DESIGN
(Great Britain)

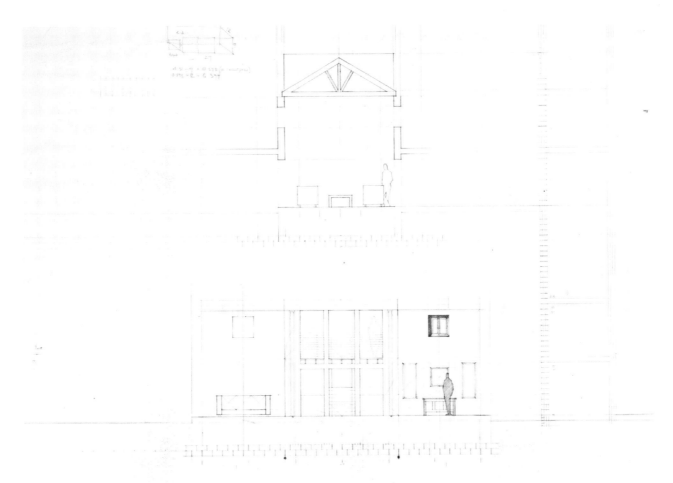

House Centred on Staircase

'. . . a house, as such, is built principally as a dwelling, as a protection against wind, rain, weather, animals, and men, and it requires a complete enclosure where a family or larger community can assemble, shut in by themselves, and pursue their needs and concerns in this seclusion. A house is an entirely purposeful structure, produced by men for human purposes. So the builder has many aims and concerns in this course of his work. In detail the frame, in order to be supported and stable, has to connect various joints and thrusts together in line with mechanical principles, and observe the conditions imposed by weight and the need for stabilising the structure, closing it, supporting its upper parts, and, in general, not merely carrying these but keeping the horizontal horizontal and binding the structure together at recesses and corners. Now a house does demand a total enclosure for which walls are the most serviceable and safest means . . . but a sort of wall can equally well be constructed from stanchions set alongside one another on which beams rest and these at the same time bind together and secure the perpendicular stanchions by which they are supported and carried. Finally, on top of these is the ceiling and the roof.'

Hegel: Aesthetics-Lectures on Fine Art

The predominance of blundering capitalist dogma and the culturally vacant acceptance of the 'house as commodity' is slowly but surely asphyxiating the real significance of the 'house as dwelling'. Architectural form and its strength as an enclosure of cultural meanings sinks deeper by the day into a quagmire of triviality, whimsy, and degenerate commerciality.

The house must be rediscovered through the essential condition surrounding its purposefulness, the availability of materials, and the honest manifestation of constructional logic. The house as a building and as a piece of architecture must 'fit' its use – not imitate or symbolise its use through concepts alien to the nature of building itself. Only through fitness can architecture satisfy the demands of purpose on the one hand whilst maintaining its own integrity as an autonomous discipline on the other.

The ground floor plan of the house is square, divided centrally and symmetrically by the staircase. A simple horizontal shift of the upper floor plan produces a colonnade at the front and a terrace at the rear. The double height entrance hall is top-lit and overlooked by the half-landing balcony; it feeds laterally into two small spaces (kitchen, breakfast room, study) which, in turn, lead into the main living space with French-doors opening onto the garden. The staircase rises and divides, giving access to four rooms, two smaller (bathroom, bedroom, study) and two larger (bedrooms).

NIGEL MILLS AND FERENCZI DESIGN
(Great Britain)

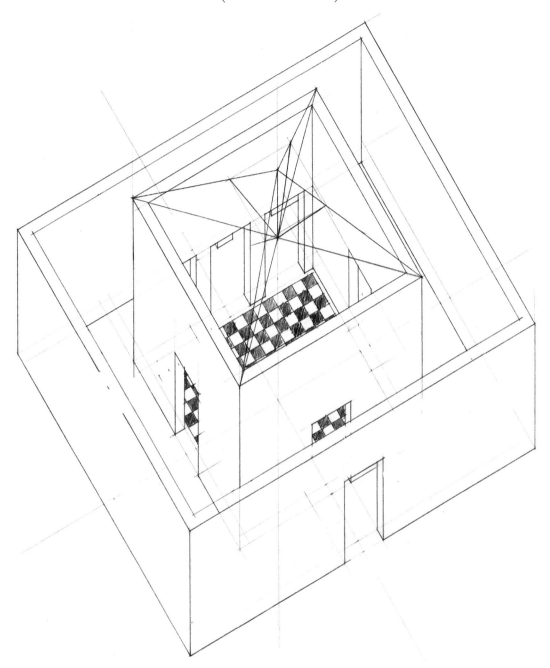

The Villa

The Villa is conceived as a simple, tranquil backdrop to human existance. It is a complete and unified entity with a clearly readable symmetrical order and spatial hierarchy, which has resisted the distortions usually caused by functional compression and restrictions of size. Through this completeness and order the house can regain its dignity as architecture. It asserts itself as a dwelling fit for human habitation, not as a profitable commodity

The villa and its garden are centered on the collective living space. This space, which is analogous in nature to the atrium of the classical Roman house, extends out into the garden through the mediating screen of the loggia. The collective space is a square of 5 metre dimension in plan and of the proportion 1:2 in section and has an exposed pyramidal timber roof structure with a central skylight.

Around the core of the central volume are a series of individual cells into which one may retreat. The larger four may be assigned to particular functions or individuals (kitchen, bedrooms, study etc), depending on whether the building is to be inhabited by an individual, couple or family. They are of a 2:3 proportion in plan and square in section. The three smaller spaces which include the vestibule, and the bathroom and cloakroom which flank it, are square in plan and of a 2:3 proportion in section.

The villa is constructed in durable masonry (brick and block) with concrete lintels explicitly spanning the openings. The walls are terminated at their apex with a simple brick cornice. The columns to the loggia are of brick with unadorned concrete capitals and are of Tuscan proportion and spacing.

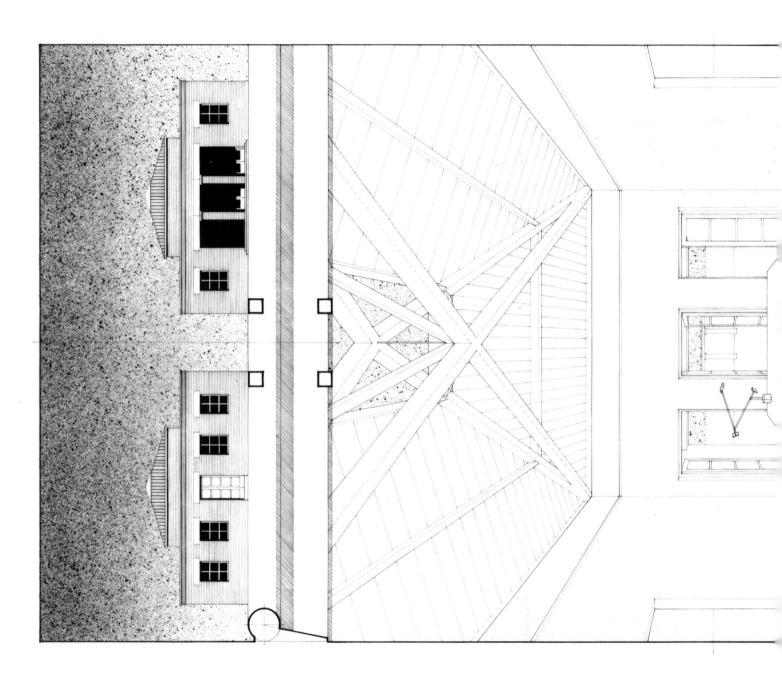

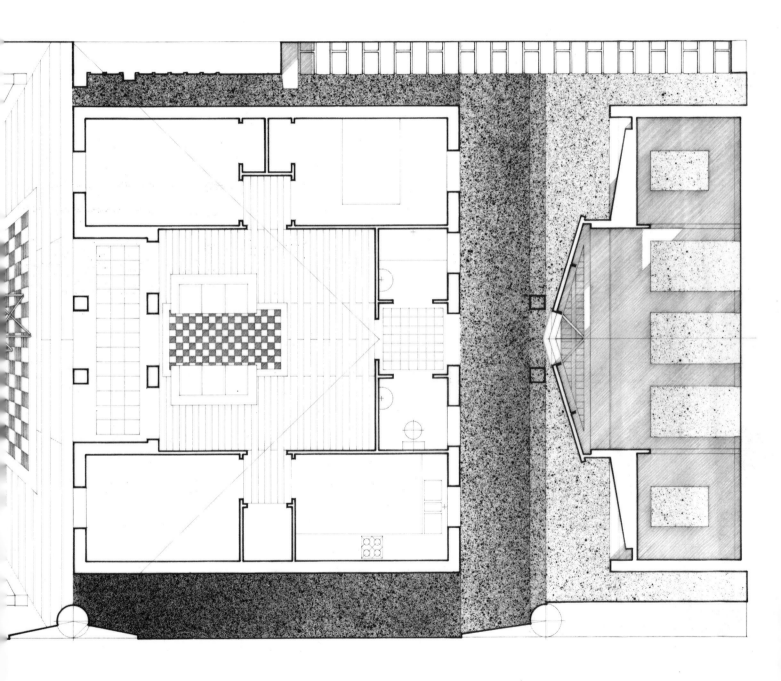

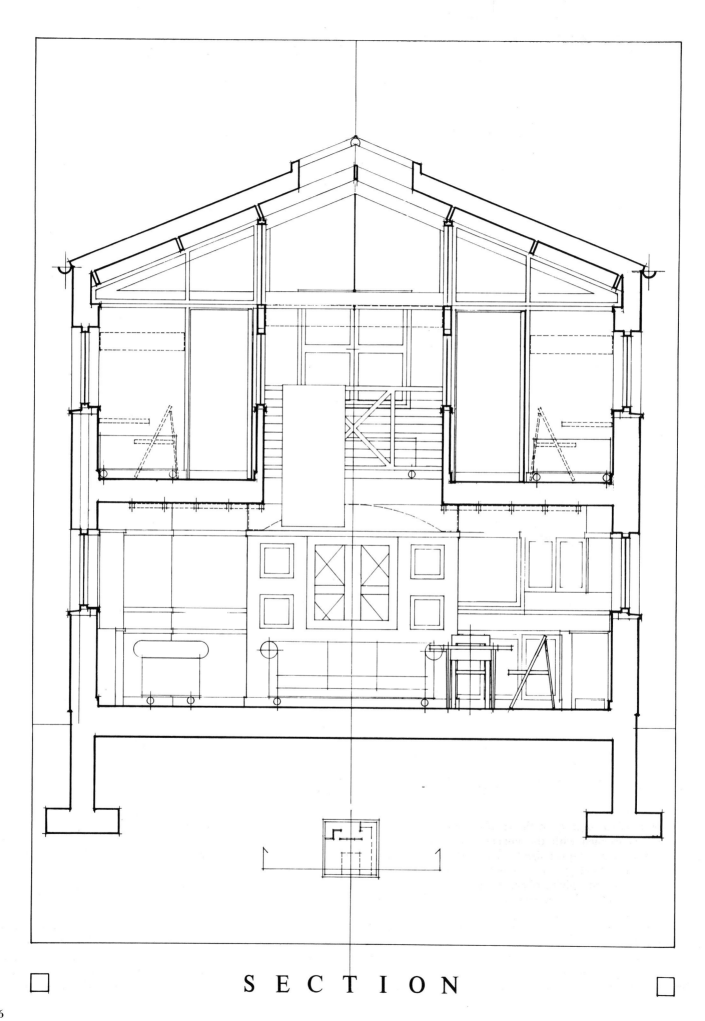

SECTION

NIGEL MILLS AND FERENCZI DESIGN
(Great Britain)

The House Centred on Living Place

It is a dream of the *dignity* of the family home. It is concerned with the normal, average and ordinary – a quiet dignity, not a dream of utopia, technology or a 'total housing solution'. It is a conspiring of concerns about the quality of the home; a constancy of aim, that a small home should be dignified and good to be in – a place for family, friends and furniture, a dog and a cat – accepting the differences, with a mutual concern and respect for living together. It is a 'mansion in miniature'; with the memory of mansion halls, bedchambers and libraries, smaller but undistorted. It combines the order of the Villa Rotunda with the flexibility of the Schröder House.

The house is a two storey economic, energy conscious form in which function and form fuse symmetrically. It centres on the space and movement of the inhabitants, functions ritualised at the edges. The ceiling plans suggest spatial division. The public face is private, the entry is signified, the hall is important, dignified and commodious. The upper floor is no longer just bedrooms; it can be used to rest, study, play, be open or private and closed. The plan also evokes other facades, responding to orientation and taste.

The house can be detached, semi-detached, terraced or formed around a courtyard and the combined strength of house and garden can order irregularities of site. The variety of plans and sections show the different independent possible configurations to choose from or adapt.

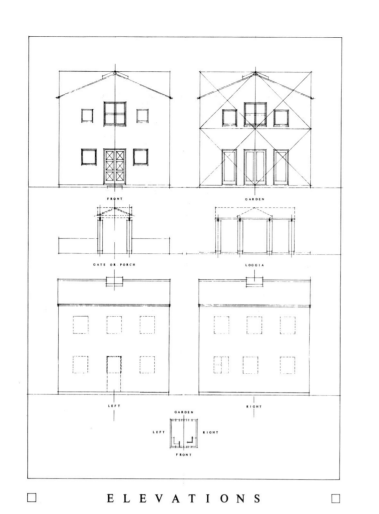

ELEVATIONS

SECTIONS

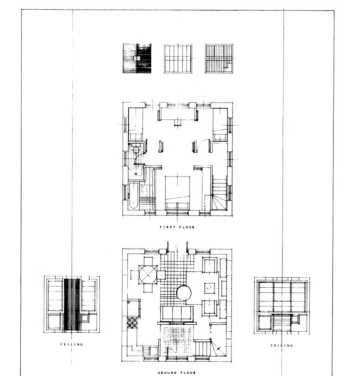

PLANS

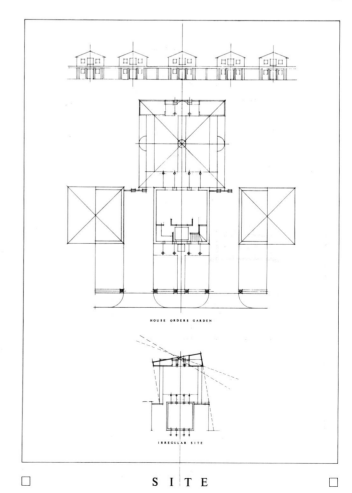

SITE

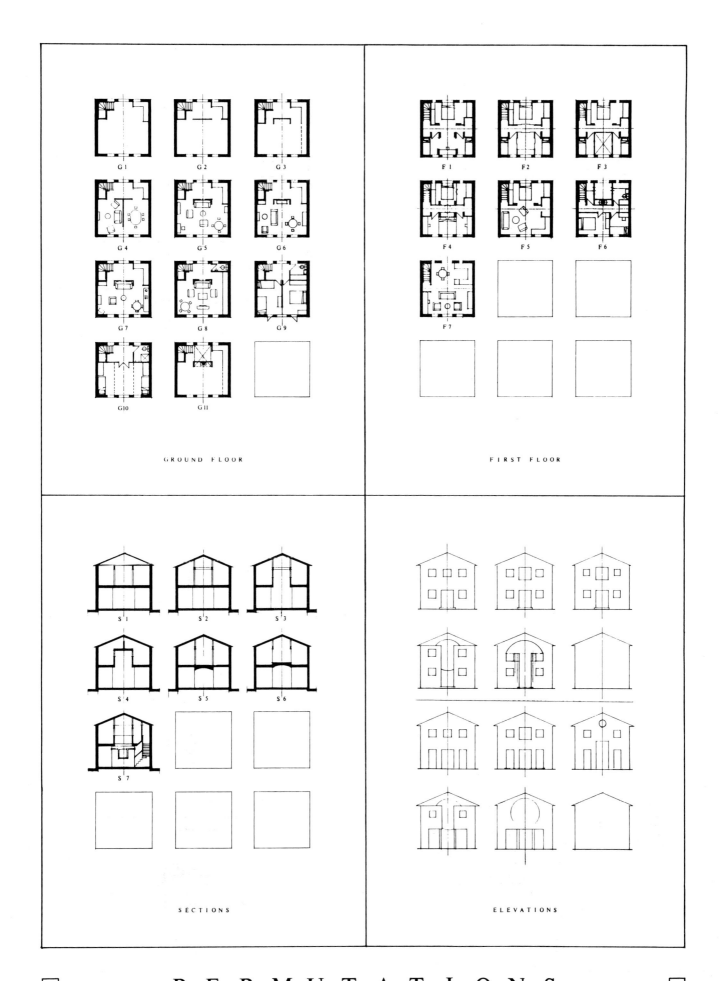

G 1   G 2   G 3

G 4   G 5   G 6

G 7   G 8   G 9

G10   G11

GROUND FLOOR

F 1   F 2   F 3

F 4   F 5   F 6

F 7

FIRST FLOOR

S 1   S 2   S 3

S 4   S 5   S 6

S 7

SECTIONS

ELEVATIONS

P E R M U T A T I O N S

MILAN S. PETKOVIĆ

(Yugoslavia)

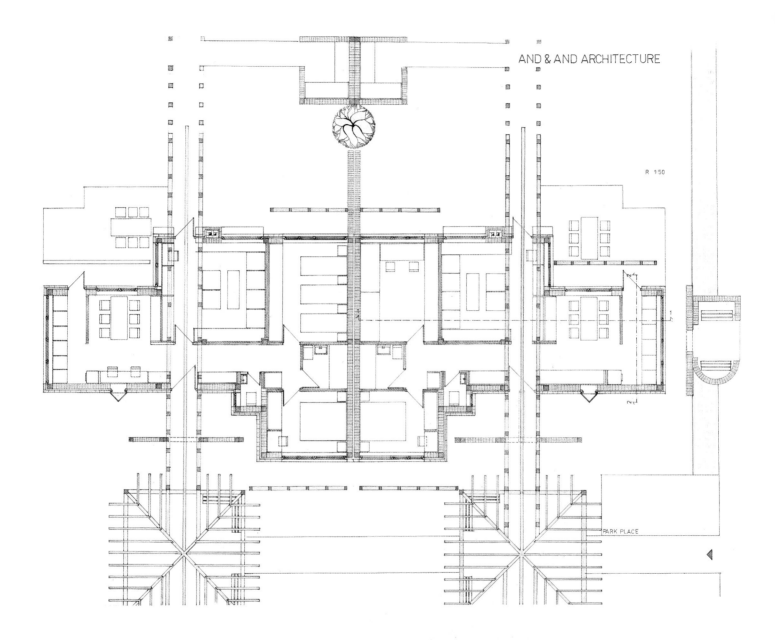

For this design project I have tried to find a new approach to architecture, one of direct physical opposition of architectural elements, expressly avoiding over-reliance on archetypal forms which I consider to be the basic weakness of Post-Modernism. The shapes, even ones in counteraction, are directly brought into space, and there, opposed at two levels: firstly, in relation to their surroundings and the designer's concept of space; secondly in relation to neighbouring architectural elements. From this, arises the interesting dynamic whereby the counterpointing itself becomes the new dimension for perceiving architecture.

I would like to point out how this approach determined the outcome of many aspects of my design.

1 Emphasis is given to the entrance – a characteristic of British architecture – by introducing a wall that does not belong to the house, either constructionally or functionally. In this instance, it has been done symmetrically with blind arcades, but many different solutions are possible.

2 The wooden lattice in front of the bedrooms serves a structural purpose, carrying the 'false roof'. Equally important is its association with classic wooden house constructions characteristic of latterday northern architecture.

3 The house has a flat roof, but as it is generally assumed that a family home should have a sloping roof, a false one has been constructed in the form of a metal grid.

4 The street wall is separated from the house providing sitting space. It belongs more to the street than the house.

5 The lantern, which begins in the 'false house' and runs throughout the house and garden, gradually decreasing in size. It is there to guide movement through the house and to divide the spaces into day and nightime areas.

6 The keystone of the front arcade wall is extended as a 'keybeam' to link the projecting wall with the house itself.

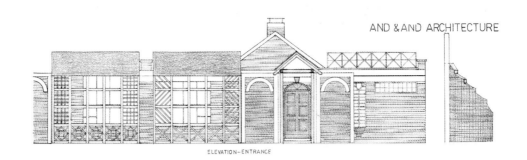

AND & AND ARCHITECTURE

ELEVATION—ENTRANCE

R 1:50

ELEVATION FROM GARDEN

VARIANCE FOR A "STREET WALL"

ELEVATION FROM LOCAL STREET

AND & AND ARCHITECTURE

1-1

2-2

FIRST CITY PARTNERSHIP
(Great Britain)

First City Partnership: Andrew Neill, Roland Way and Ian Holland

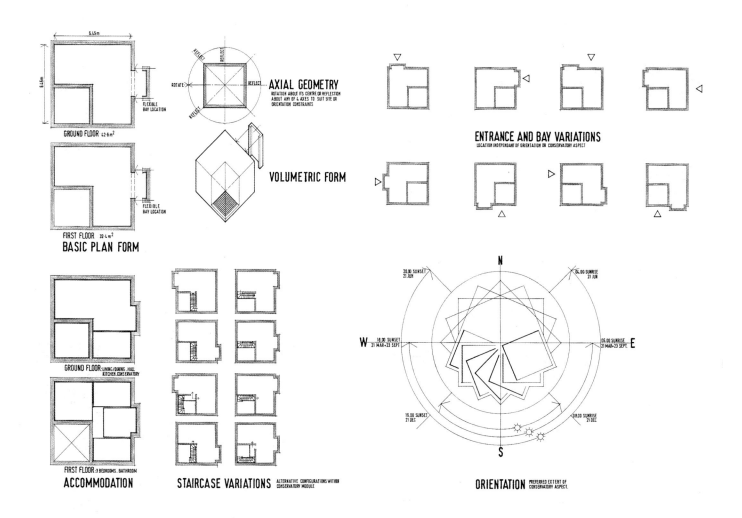

Our aim was to develop a general plan module that could encompass, within its frame, many variations to meet various needs and site constraints. For a single plan form to fulfill such criteria, a strong underlying geometry must be established, because any formal attempt to meet universal site variations must be based upon a sufficiently coherent geometry to allow for a multiplicity of possibilities. In response we have developed a square plan form which can not only be rotated about its centre, but can also be reflected about any one of four axes.

The structural fabric of the house is wholly independent of internal partitioning, which allows total flexibility when planning ground and first floor accommodation. Traditionally, the 50%-50% split between ground and first floors dictates that sleeping accommodation will equal living accommodation. We aimed to reduce sleeping accommodation to the minimum to allow us to increase the living space substantially within the overall requirements of 75m², by using the full square plan at ground floor level, but only three quarters of this plan area on first floor. This gives an area of 42.6m² at ground floor, with 32.3m² above, creating a double height space which serves two functions: a) vertical circulation; b) conservatory. Locating vertical circulation within this space allows unhindered free planning of the first floor. The staircase fits the quarter-module and can be rotated to suit the situation.

This plan has an inherent flexibility which allows not only a selection of ground and first floor variations, but also a selection of elevational treatments which can be used wholly independently of plan type to suit urban or rural locations. To capitalise on this concept and exploit it to the full, we feel that development would need to be put into programming the system for CAD usage. This would allow the designer to select appropriate combinations of ground and first floor plans from the full range of options available, and pick from a 'pattern book' of traditional facade components.

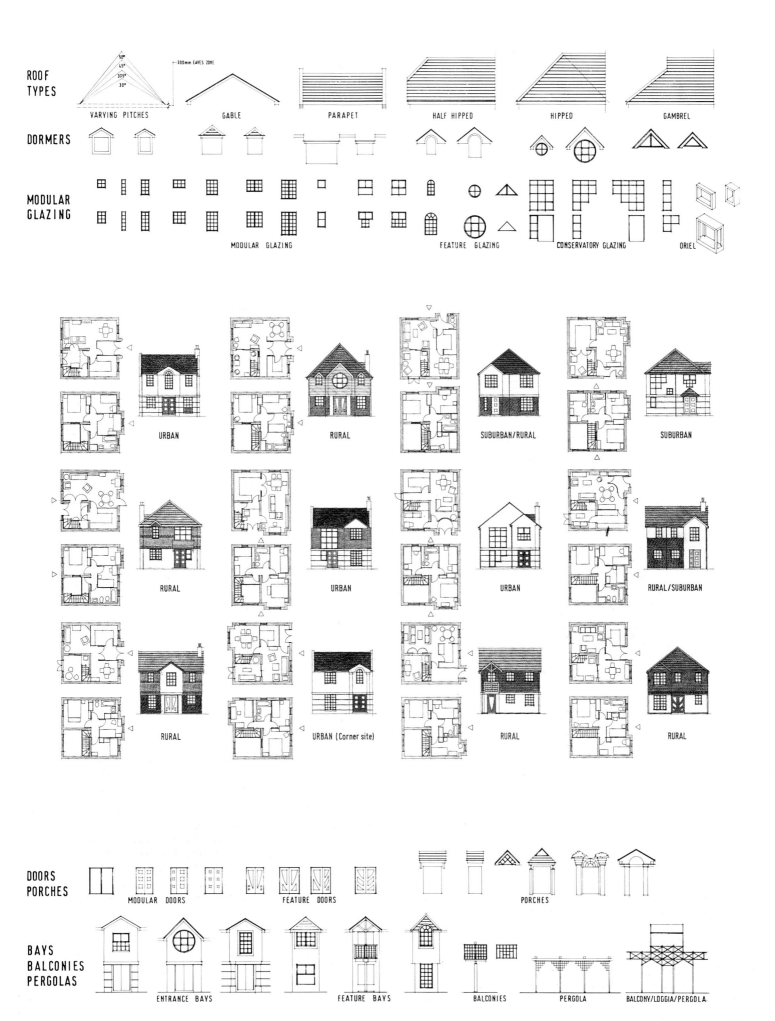

ROOF TYPES

VARYING PITCHES   GABLE   PARAPET   HALF HIPPED   HIPPED   GAMBREL

300mm EAVES ZONE

DORMERS

MODULAR GLAZING

MODULAR GLAZING   FEATURE GLAZING   CONSERVATORY GLAZING   ORIEL

URBAN   RURAL   SUBURBAN/RURAL   SUBURBAN

RURAL   URBAN   URBAN   RURAL/SUBURBAN

RURAL   URBAN (Corner site)   RURAL   RURAL

DOORS PORCHES

MODULAR DOORS   FEATURE DOORS   PORCHES

BAYS BALCONIES PERGOLAS

ENTRANCE BAYS   FEATURE BAYS   BALCONIES   PERGOLA   BALCONY/LOGGIA/PERGOLA.

23

ZHANG JIAN, GAO QI + LUO XING
(China)

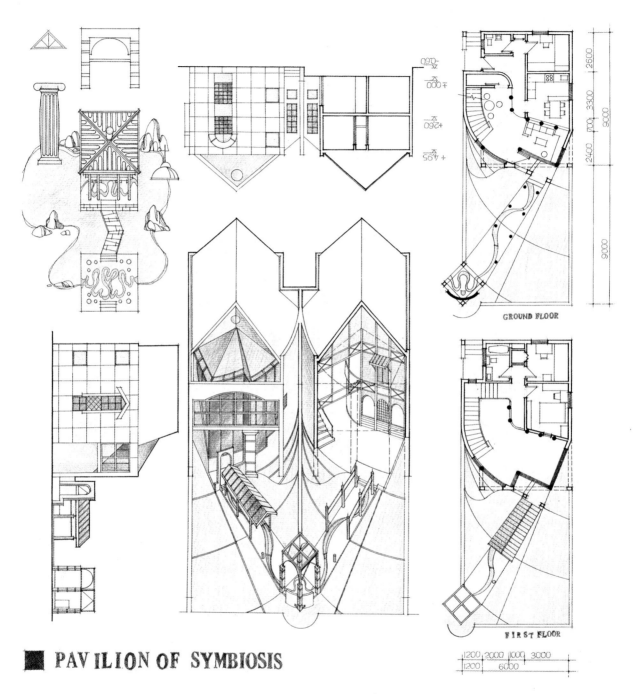

PAVILION OF SYMBIOSIS

Nowadays, we live in such a multi-dimensional society that people feel torn between old and new ideas. Our project aims to create an intermediary space, flexible yet lively, to accommodate these different ideas. The function of inserting a third space, the intermediary space, into the designed architectural space, is to create a kind of co-existence between the building and its surroundings – in this case, using the pavilion, the corridor and the garden. The stream meandering through the garden not only connects the living space to the external environment, but also encourages neighbourliness by providing a link rather than a solid barrier between houses.

This idea of co-existence is emphasized as an essential element, consciously combining very different features to create a variety of meanings. By using traditional structures and modern techniques, we hope to create a new meaning, to see history and development, man and technology side by side rather than in opposition.

At the beginning of the 18th century, British architects were fascinated by the art of Chinese gardening. At the same time, Chinese architects were also influenced by traditional British architecture. Today's society calls for an understanding and co-existence of different cultures. We hope that the Chinese approach to spatial treatment can find its way into the development of modern British housing, as a means of creating a new concept of space.

BO HELLIWELL
(Canada)

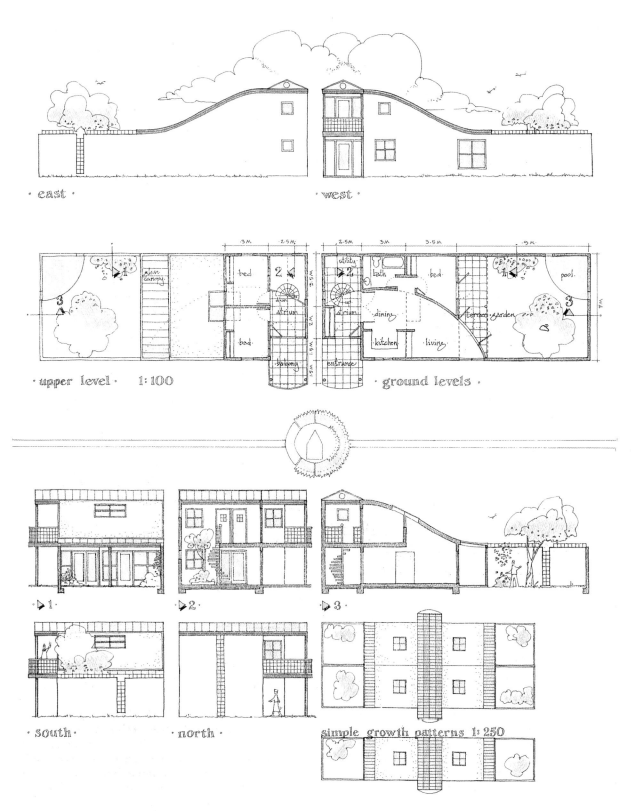

· east ·

· west ·

· upper level ·   1:100

· ground levels ·

▷1   ▷2   ▷3

· south ·   · north ·   simple growth patterns 1:250

Gentle lines embrace the inhabitants. There is excitement in the spaces: some are low and sheltering; others reach for light. A wall curves through the house from atrium to terrace, dramatically connecting the inner and outer gardens. The glass roof allows sunlight to penetrate the atrium; its warmth can be circulated to help heat. Rooms open into this space. The outer walls define a simple plan, yet give this house its graceful form. The roof appears complex yet its construction is a simple span. In fact, there is nothing extraordinary about the construction. Common building parts will do.

TOMÁŠ PROUZA

(Czechoslovakia)

I have chosen to design a house which takes full account of the changing needs of a family, from when there are young children, through teenagers, to when the children have left home.

Since the owners and most permanent inhabitants of the house are the parents it seems only fair that the first floor should be given over to them, whilst the children will undoubtedly appreciate a more independant position on the ground floor. The large children's room, 16.6m², could easily be divided in two, if necessary. Apart from catering for the individual's needs, my main emphasis was the living room, which together with the kitchen, dining room and stairs, is almost 30m², and 3.9m high at the crest. A second staircase leads down to the garden and serves as an emergency exit.

Additional storage space for bicycles, pram, garden tools and firewood has been provided under both staircases and on the balcony. I felt it was better and cheaper to house the garage under the same roof rather that to build an extension for this purpose.

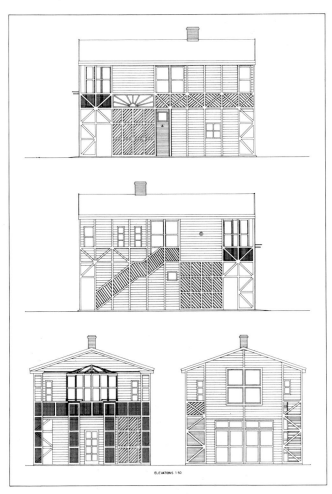

ELEVATIONS 1:50

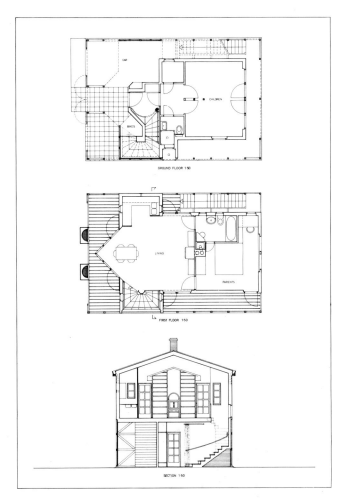

GROUND FLOOR 1:50

FIRST FLOOR 1:50

SECTION 1:50

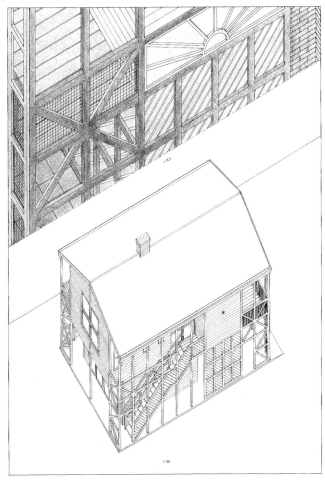

1:50

ANDREJ KOCJAN
(Yugoslavia)

The main idea of my concept is the production of the architectural types by a process chosen in advance, in which the architect does not transform one single archetype – the most usual method nowadays – but from one known archetype, he captures the essence of an entirely new one. The main element of transformation is the artist's creativity; the emergence of the new product does not abstract or purify new elementary symbolical values, on the contrary it creates new symbols by analogy, producing further spatial orders from the existing primary elements of the basic type.

The terrace house represents the choice of that architectural type which should serve as a basis for the production of other types by its elementary regularity of space and symbol. The search for that regularity in the development of the English terrace house suggests a methodical attitude in

which the abstraction of those principals functions as the essential element of shaping. I have chosen to illustrate the compositional process with the analogy of a chess game. The final stage of this abstraction resembles a Sicilian opening move, where the choice of move itself represents a certain subjective criterion whose rules are yet known and accurately determined.

The basic principles of the composition in the concept of the terrace house are the longitudinal emphasis and caricaturing narrowness. However, the elements of the composition are the typical archetypal elements of a terrace house: a narrow, high street facade, an entrance portal, a mullion window and archetypal elements of the house in general: a fireside with a chimney acting simultaneously as a column, a representative staircase, and a cupola illuminating a sitting room at the centre of the house. The longitudinal and narrow emph-

ases act an important part in the urban scheme of the building concerning its rational and economic meaning as well as the redefinition of the outer public space.

The next step in transforming the basic archetype moves the 'bishops' and 'castles' forward to create the detached house – an 'English mansion in miniature' – with the emergence of the wings (or sides) of the house. The semi-detached house which follows on from this, is a hybrid – a cross between the longitudinal and central archetypes, in which the archetype itself no longer exists, but is merely the memory of two possibilities out of which it could be born.

Lastly, the 'Strada Bellissima' represents the apogee of all these forms rolled into one street – an explosion of architectural creativity offering the richness of all these transformations side by side.

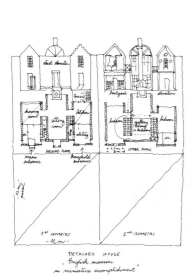

DETACHED HOUSE
"English mansion
in miniature accomplishment"

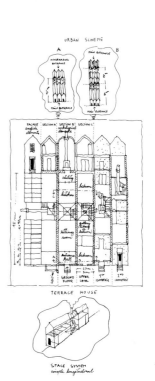

JOHN SIMPSON & PARTNERS
(Great Britain)

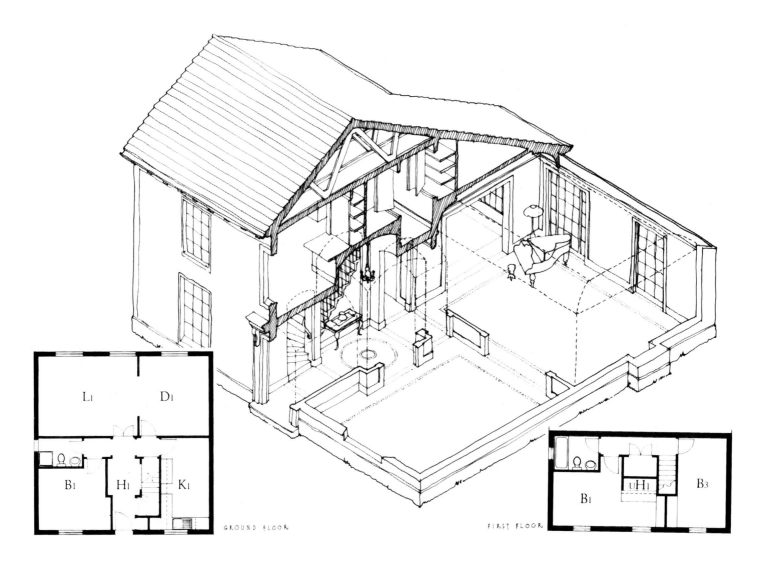

L1　D1

B1　H1　K1

GROUND FLOOR

B1　uH1　B3

FIRST FLOOR

Inherent in the characteristics of the design system, is a degree of variation that in normal circumstances would be considered economically prohibitive. Here, despite the apparent variation, each and every house type can have identical staircases with identical detailing arrangements, identical bathrooms with identical plumbing arrangements, identical kitchen layouts with sink and washing machine outlets, and so on. These features have little or no effect on the user but will make construction easier without sacrificing the variety in house types. The potential cost saving here, is not only in the standardisation of components and site administration, but also, in any increase in productivity associated with a reduction of wasted time and delays on site, due to unnecessary different designs and components. This time and cost saving means that more effort can be spent refining the smaller design details, to improve the quality and convenience of the design for the inhabitants which in the case of the elderly or the handicapped, can be of paramount importance. Here, specific standards and requirements can be built into the design of the components. These can then be used from one development to the next, ensuring a continuity of guaranteed standards and performance. An important further advantage, which is not normally available in building, is that modification and fine tuning of details can take place in light of experience from previous developments. In time, more components can be added to the basic set so that a flexible and interchangeable collection is built-up. The external appearance and materials would be designed separately to suit the local conditions and traditions.

When preparing a design brief, the cost implications of each of the requirements is never fully realized, until a complete design is put together. An important advantage of this approach, is that the relative cost implication of each of the requirements can be quantified and, therefore, the balance in the design sorted out at component level, in advance, before a single development is begun.

The system is also particularly well suited to computer-aided design. The component plans are designed based on a chosen structural span, a construction system and particular controlling dimensions. Each component is then developed into a partial working drawing which is input into the computer together with all relevant information, down to door hinges and pipe bends. The system is extremely versatile, not only in plan form and layout, but also, in built form and appearance.

A SMALL VILLA OF 78 SQUARE METRES

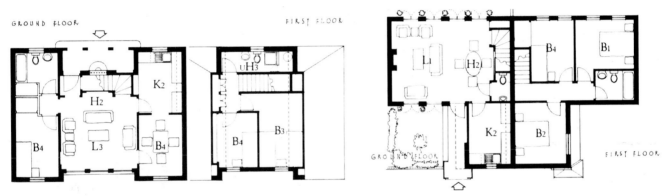

A TERRACED HOUSE OF 77 SQUARE METRES

MICHAEL HANUSCAK, JURAJ KARASEK +EDUARD KOLEK
(Czechoslovakia)

Our design for a two-storey housetype is based on maximum space and area economy. The total floor area is only 75m² – although we have combined the space between both storeys in the entrance hall and nearby staircase. If additional space is needed for a fifth member of the family, this two-storey hall can be easily transformed into a small third bedroom.

The interior measurements of the house are based on a horizontal and vertical module of 90cm – thus 4.50m x 9m with a ceiling height of 2.70m. The construction width for all three variants of the terraced house is 4.80m. This allows maximum urban economy within a site only 4.80m wide. Flexibility of orientation is allowed for by alternating those rooms on opposite sides of the cross axis of the house.

The basic housetype is the terrace house type 'A'. On the ground floor there is a one space living room organised around a fireplace. House type 'B' has a void above the central part of the living room, overlooked by single French windows from the bedrooms. It is lit from above by a skylight. Type 'C' has an open courtyard at its centre – but this can easily be roofed over with a glass skylight if required.

The semi-detached house may be formed from all three types mentioned, but we recommend using types 'B' and 'C'. Likewise, the detached house can be based on any of the three house types – again we would recommend using type 'C'.

The heating system is based on a combination of traditional central heating (probably gas-fired, with the boiler on the first floor in the bathroom) and passive solar heating from the conservatory to supplement the open fires in the living/sitting rooms. This combination entails minimum direct heating in spring and autumn. It is also possible to combine traditional central heating with active solar heating but this necessitates water storage tanks below ground floor.

The simple masonry construction is completed by uniform sash windows (on the south side these can be replaced by small conservatories), prefabricated concrete columns, chimneys and horizontal constructions based on a 4.50m inner module. This strict module unification helps to keep the house at a modest price.

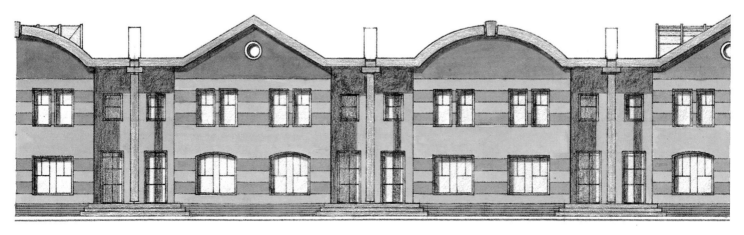

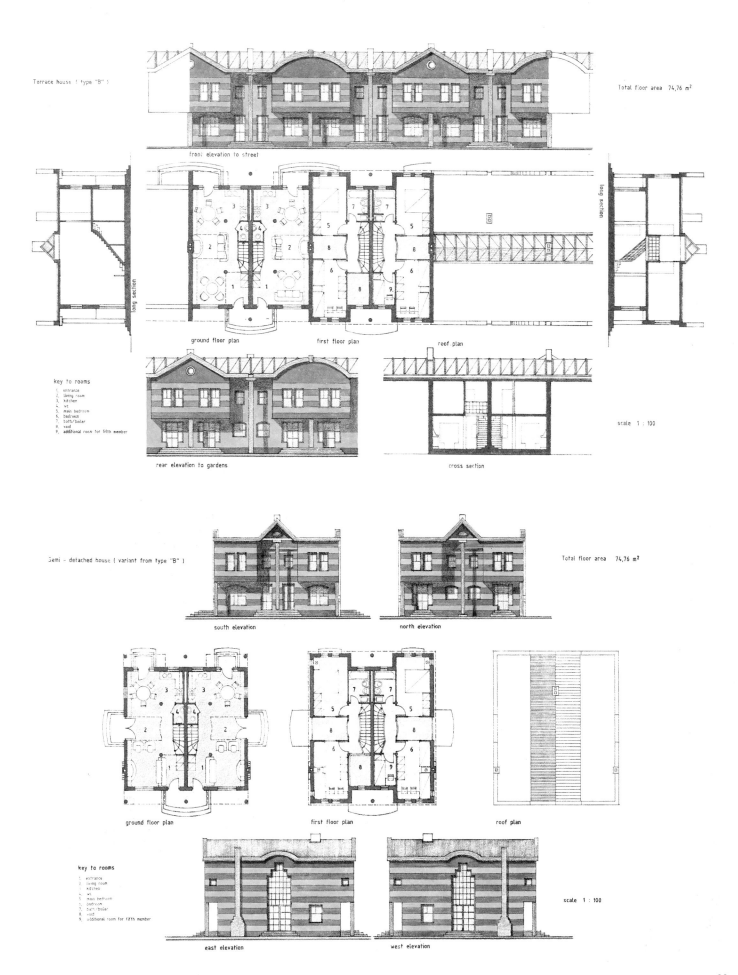

Terrace house (type "B")

Total floor area 74,76 m²

front elevation to street

long section

long section

ground floor plan

first floor plan

roof plan

key to rooms

1. entrance
2. living room
3. kitchen
4. wc
5. main bedroom
6. bedroom
7. bath/boiler
8. void
9. additional room for fifth member

rear elevation to gardens

cross section

scale 1 : 100

Semi - detached house (variant from type "B")

Total floor area 74,76 m²

south elevation

north elevation

ground floor plan

first floor plan

roof plan

key to rooms

1. entrance
2. living room
3. kitchen
4. wc
5. main bedroom
6. bedroom
7. bath/boiler
8. void
9. additional room for fifth member

east elevation

west elevation

scale 1 : 100

33

DMITRY A. WELICHKIN, ALEXANDER A. BELAEV + VADIM A. LEVY

(USSR)

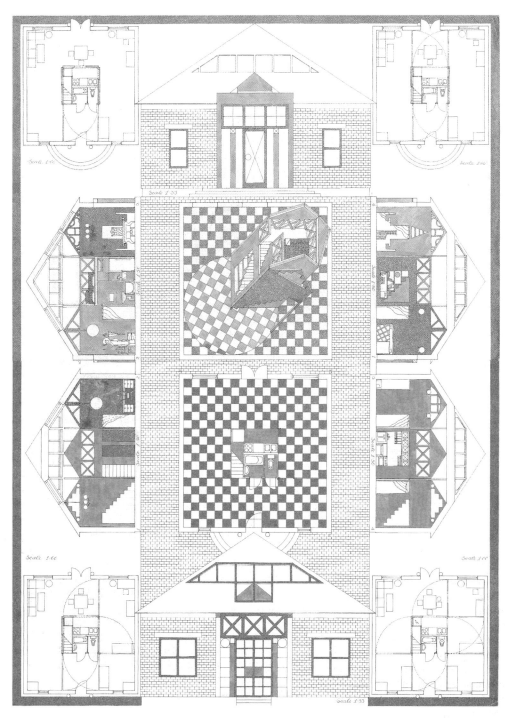

This residential building consists of two parts, the brick shell with a wooden roof and the central core of reinforced concrete with pivoted wooden partitions, where all the necessary facilities (kitchen, WC, etc) are installed. A steep staircase leads to the top level where a master bedroom is situated. The pivoting partitions allow the inner space to be adapted for the use by 2 to 5 members of a family, creating different kinds of spaces, from a detached 'Red Tower', when closed, to a classic suite of rooms if necessary. The variously decorated partitions allow for the creation of interiors suitable to each member of the family.

Entrance foyer and master bedroom are naturally lit by transparent skylights. Likewise the rest of the rooms, excluding WC, are also lit by skylights or four windows. The total floor area is 75m². The design is devised on a 3 meter square grid.

We were eager to do away with a rigid internal plan and to produce a house that reveals itself only to its inhabitants.

ANDREI CHELTSOV + MIKHAIL LABAZOV
(USSR)

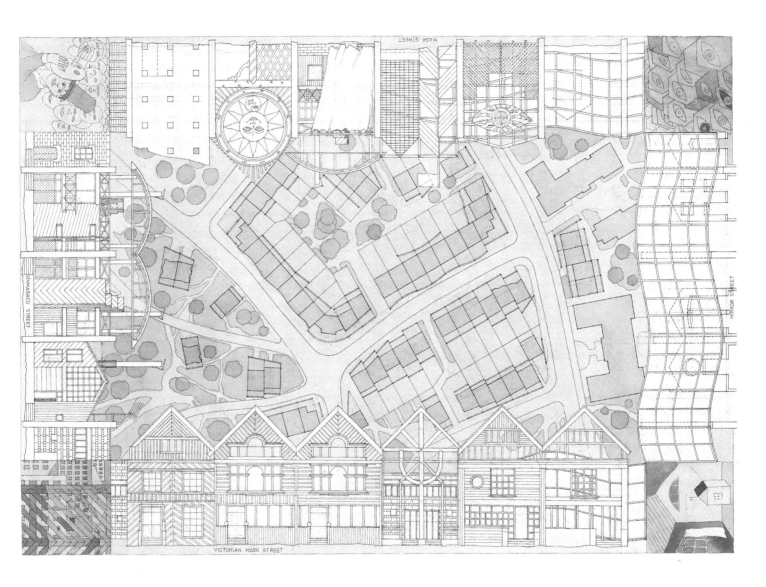

The main problem we have tried to solve is the contradiction between the personal nature of the house and the social nature of the building industry. Inside a separate inner, 'decorative' house, we have designed a social area that is the face of the family and the key to the understanding of the house. The inner house is freely movable and can be positioned in a variety of ways within the big house, depending on the wishes of the customer.

The big house consists of two longitudinal supporting constructions (6.3 metres apart). The permanent face of the big house can be of stone, brick, wooden panelling or glass, through which the inner house can be seen.

The next step is the creation with the aid of transparent masks of a buffer zone between the individual and society, between the big house and the street. The buffer masks can be made out of narrow wooden boards, pieces of plastic or metal, or of solar panels, and represent a second facade concealing the real face of the house. Paintings can be drawn on the inside of the masks, and these will be seen superimposed on the city outside.

Our house is a construction site for the inhabitant. It is today's house for tommorrow. As the family grows and its income grows, the cultural needs of the inhabitants change, and our house is adaptable to all these alterations. The house can alter both its external form and its internal content by changing its decorative inner

house, its facade and buffer mask. The buffer reserves a zone for further extensions to the house or can be used for other functions, such as greenhouses, ecological systems, wind turbines, etc.

Apart from individual inner houses, facades and masks, we also examine the possibility of individual design in each specific case. The individual approach naturally makes the house more expensive, but with the increasing use of highly productive computers in design and construction and the automation of manual labour on the building site, construction is becoming cheaper all the time. What is more, there are a limited number of elements in the proposed system.

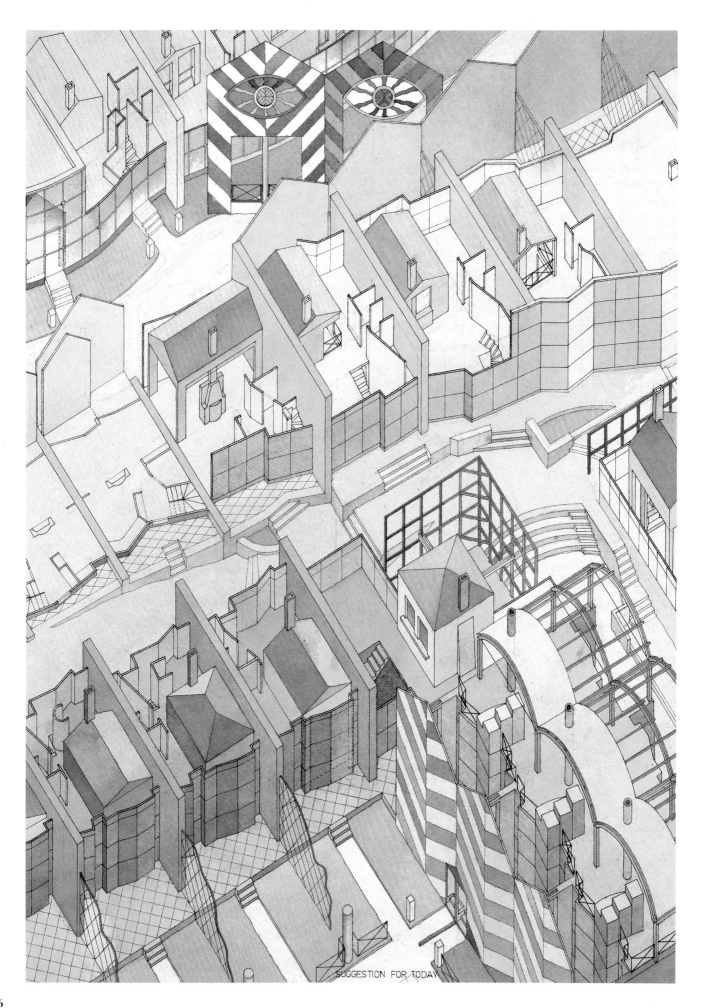

SUGGESTION FOR TODAY

elevation 1:50

plan 1

plan 2

1:100
S 75m²

section 1:50

A SELECTION OF
UNPREMIATED ENTRIES

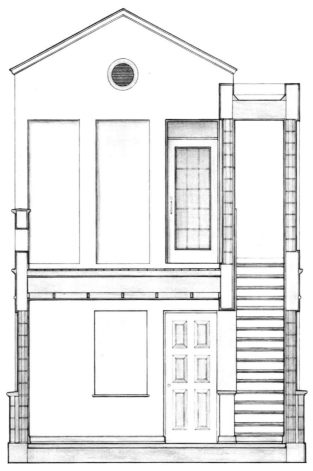

Michael Paul Vascellaro (USA): Stucco mouldings add flourish to
the simple order of this unashamedly eclectic entry.

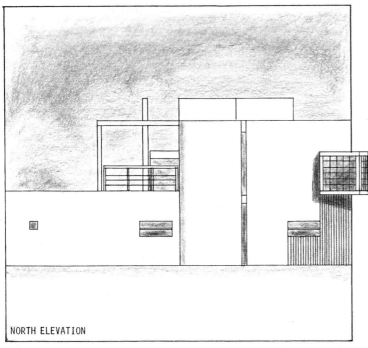

NORTH ELEVATION

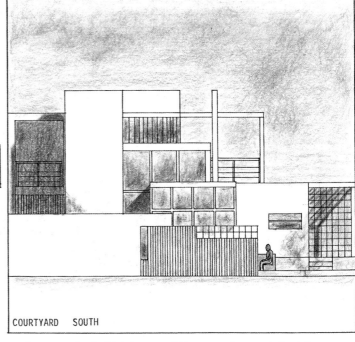

COURTYARD SOUTH

Tuula Sipinen (Finland): Using an environment simulator to plan a complete environment from street-level, this is just one of 28 permutations on the basic house type
put forward in a vast submission by architectural students at Tampere University of Technology.

Elgar Godinho (Portugal): No amount of re-jigging could bring true classical order to this impractical but charmingly drawn entry.

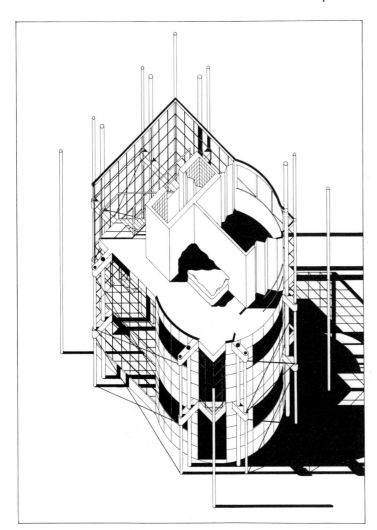

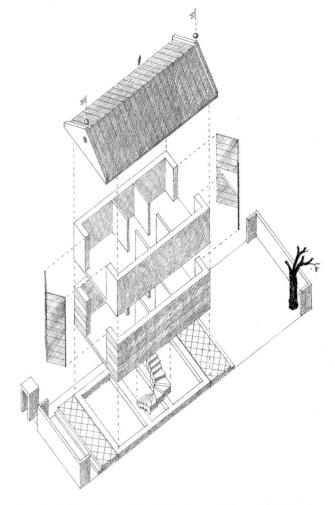

Pratik Desau (Great Britain): Purporting to be an investigation into the authenticity of High-Tech, this submission also attempts a visual distinction between 'house' and 'home'.

Andreas Meck (Great Britain): A playful scheme, this Box of Bricks is a 'house for today' game kit which can be assembled in a number of ways to meet a wide range of different situations and environments.

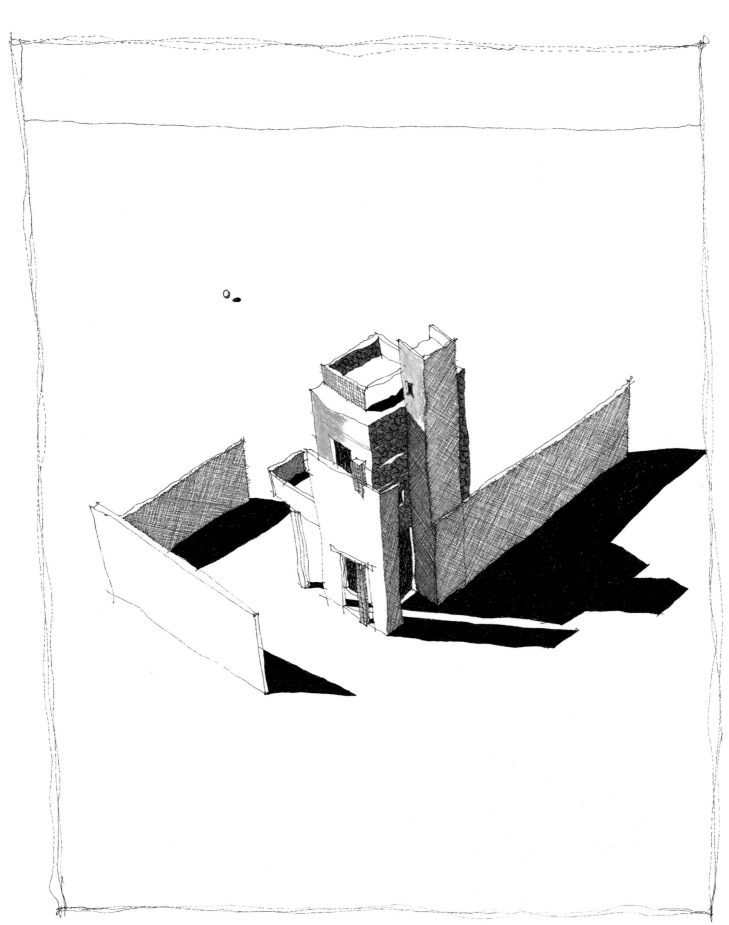

Craig J Moller (New Zealand): The design seeks to explore the interplay of interior living spaces, expressed as volumes, with planar walls defining exterior spaces.

Exteriorized style

Ecologist style

Eduardo Carqueijeiro (Portugal): Two of the more recognisable 'living styles' to which this 'highly personalised house' can be adapted.

Dolgoi, Nekrassov, Rebrov, Stepanov and Vihodtcev (USSR): 'A House with Two Faces' offers its public aspect to tradition, allowing its garden facade free-rein with unspecified contemporary styles.

N F Saunders (Mexico): The range of facade details offered here all draw heavily upon the suburban vernacular to underline their context.

Brodsky & Utkin (USSR): A surprisingly nostalgic but beautifully drawn evocation of an old-fashioned home within a low-cost, modern shell.

Tom Knott (Great Britain): The Ribbon House is draped with a colourful screen of woven PVC strips alternately held away from the glazing on metal brackets or left loose to flap in the wind, creating variously shaped openings and changing light effects throughout the day.